Basic Beliefs

BASIC BELIEFS

A Woman's Workshop on the Christian Faith

Carolyn Nystrom

Lamplighter Books Grand Rapids, Michigan
Zondervan Publishing House

BASIC BELIEFS: A WOMAN'S WORKSHOP ON THE
   CHRISTIAN FAITH
Copyright © 1986 by Carolyn Nystrom

Lamplighter Books are published by Zondervan
Publishing House, 1415 Lake Drive, S.E.,
Grand Rapids, Michigan 49506

This book was previously published under the title:
   New Life: A Woman's Workshop on Salvation
Copyright © 1983 by The Zondervan Corporation
Grand Rapids, Michigan

Library of Congress Cataloging in Publication Data

Nystrom, Carolyn.
   Basic Beliefs.

   Previously published as: New life: a woman's workshop on
salvation. c1983.
   "A Zondervan publication"—Cover p. 4.
   1. Women—Religious life.   2. Salvation.   I. Title.
BV4527.N87   1986   230'.076   86-28070
ISBN 0-310-41971-9 (pbk.)

Printed in the United States of America

86   87   88   89   90   91 / ZO / 9   8   7   6   5   4   3   2

CONTENTS

BASIC BELIEFS

"I don't know what I believe any more—maybe nothing at all," my friend stated flatly. "I want to believe, at least sometimes I do, but the more questions I ask, the fewer answers I find."

I made noises that meant, "I'm listening; go on."

"I feel like I'm in a lifeboat in the ocean with no land on any horizon. Should I bother to paddle? If so, in what direction?"

We talked for a long time. My friend's question-list was indeed impressive: Who is God? Who am I? Why am I here? Why pray? Is the Bible true—any of it? All of it? Is it presumptuous to think Christian beliefs are more valid than other world religions? What is real, in matters of faith? And what is mere wishful thinking? What about feelings? If it works and feels right, does that make it true—at least for me? And the church: how can that motley crew of human fallibility have any connection to God?

I didn't have a solid set of answers to give my friend—just some general compass markings that might point to land beyond the horizon. But as we closed our conversation, one suggestion came to my mind that might help my friend untangle those wadded snarls of doubt. Was there a hidden core of belief somewhere inside?

"Why don't you stop the questions, just for a few moments," I suggested. "Try to focus for those moments on what you *do* believe. Then write a list of those basic beliefs— and the evidence for each. After that, let's talk again."

And we did, over and over: by letter, by phone, in person. And many of the questions are still just that—questions. Perhaps one day, the answer list will begin to grow.

But the reason I gave my friend the writing assignment was because the Christian faith grows out of a small cluster of basic beliefs. True, we can visit whole libraries devoted to the minutia of Christian theology. Yet, at bottom, only a few major tenets form a foundation from which this wealth springs. And the root system for that structure of beliefs is Scripture itself: a fifteen-hundred page tome written over a nearly two-thousand-year period, yet possessing astounding internal harmony. Therefore, it's entirely appropriate that a study of basic beliefs would have a study of Scripture as its foundation.

And what are the beliefs that make the Christian faith unique? We are soon back to the set of questions that plagued my friend: Who is God? Who are we as human beings? How does one relate to the other? What does God expect from me? When does life begin—and end? How can I grow?

And as evidence that our compass is aimed in the right direction, we must also ask, does Scripture coincide with our experience?

Basic beliefs. Well worth some careful probing. Because all of eternity is at stake.

I'VE JOINED THE GROUP. NOW WHAT?

You've joined a group of people who agree that the Bible is worth studying. For some it is the Word of God and therefore a standard for day-to-day decisions. Others may say the Bible is a collection of interesting teachings and tales, worthy of time and interest but not much more. You may place yourself at one end of this spectrum or at the other end. Or you may fit somewhere in between. But you have one goal in common with the other people in your group: you believe that the Bible is worth your time, and you hope to enjoy studying it together.

To meet this goal, a few simple guidelines will prevent needless problems.

1. Take a Bible with you. Any modern translation is fine. Suggested versions include: Revised Standard Version, New American Standard Bible, Today's English Version, New International Version, Jerusalem Bible, New American Bible.

A few versions, however, do not work well in group Bible study. For beautiful language, the King James Version is unsurpassed. Yours may bear great sentimental value because it belonged to your grandmother. But if you use a King James, you will spend a great deal of effort translating the Elizabethan English into today's phrasing, perhaps losing valuable meaning in the process.

Paraphrases like Living Bible, Phillips, Amplified, Reader's Digest Bible, and New King James Bible are especially helpful in private devotions, but they lack the accuracy of a translation by Bible scholars. Therefore leave these at home on Bible study day.

Two versions deserve special consideration. The New International Version matches the phrasing of questions in this guide. Today's English Version is an easy-to-read translation, just right for the person who has always thought that the Bible is hard to understand.

2. Arrive at Bible study on time. You'll feel as if you're half a step behind throughout the session if you miss the Bible readings and the opening questions.

3. Come prepared. Some people have trouble concentrating on a Scripture passage if they read it for the first time during a group discussion. If you fall into that category, read the passage ahead of time while you are alone. But try to reserve final decisions about its meaning until you've had a chance to discuss it with the group.

4. Call your hostess if you are going to be absent. This saves her setting a place for you if refreshments are served. It also frees the group to begin on time without waiting needlessly for you.

When you miss a group session, study the passage

independently. You'll feel better able to participate when you return if you have studied the intervening material.

5. Volunteer to be a hostess. A quick way to feel that you belong to this Bible study group is to have the group meet at your house.

6. Decide if you are a talker or a listener. This is a discussion Bible study, and for a discussion to work well, all persons should participate more or less equally.

If you're a talker, count to ten before you speak. Try waiting until several people speak before you give your point of view.

If you're a listener, remind yourself that just as you benefit from what others say, they profit from your ideas. Besides, your insights will mean more even to you if you put them into words and say them aloud. So take courage and speak.

7. Keep on track. This is a group responsibility. Remember that you are studying the basic beliefs of the Christian faith. Although a speech, magazine article, or book may relate to the topic, don't bring it into the discussion; it will automatically take time away from the main object of your study: looking at Scripture. In the process, the whole group may go off onto an interesting but time-consuming tangent, thereby making the leader's job more difficult.

Most of the discussions in this guide focus on a single passage of Scripture. As a courtesy to the group members who are less familiar with all of Scripture, try to limit each day's discussion to the designated passage. Besides, a concentrated examination of one section of the Bible will reveal more than you ever thought possible. Naturally, once you've studied a section as a group, you may refer to it at will.

8. Help pace the study. With the questions and your Bible in front of you, you can be aware of whether the study is progressing at an adequate pace. Each group member shares the responsibility of seeing that the entire passage is covered and the study is brought to a profitable close.

9. Don't criticize another church or religion. You might find that the quiet person across the table attends that church—and she won't be back to your group.

10. Get to know people in your group. Call each other during the week, between meetings. Meet socially, share a car pool when convenient, offer to take a meal to an ill group member. You may discover that you have more in common than a willingness to study the Bible. Perhaps you'll add to your list of friends.

11. Invite others to the group. Any Bible study group grows best as it absorbs new people and new ideas. So share your new-found interest with a friend or neighbor.

12. Get ready to lead. It doesn't take a mature Bible student to lead this study. Just asking the questions in this guide should prompt a thorough digging into the passage. Besides, you'll find a hefty section of leader's notes in the back of this guide in case you feel a little insecure. So once you've attended the group a few times, sign up to lead a discussion. Remember, the leader learns more than anyone else.

ME, A LEADER?

Sure. Many Bible study groups have the members share the responsibility of leading the discussion. Sooner or later your turn will come. Here are a few pointers to quell any rising panic and help you keep the group members working together toward their common goal.

1. Prepare well ahead of time. A week or two in advance is not too much. Read the Scripture passage every day for several successive days. Go over the questions, writing out possible answers in your book. Check the Leader's Helps at the back of the book for additional ideas, then read the questions again—several times—until the sequence and wording seem natural to you. Don't let yourself be caught during the study with that I-wonder-what-comes-next feeling. Take careful note of the major area of application. Try living it for a week. By then you will discover some of the difficulties others in your group will face when they try to do the same. Finally, pray. Ask God to lead you as you lead the group. Ask Him to make you sensitive to people, to the Scripture, and to Himself. Expect to grow. You will.

2. Pace the study. Begin on time. People have come to study the Bible. You don't need to apologize for that. At the appointed hour, simply announce that it's time to begin, open with prayer, and launch into the study.

Keep an eye on the clock throughout the study. These questions are geared to last for an hour to an hour and fifteen minutes. Don't spend forty-five minutes on the first three questions and then rush through the rest.

On the other hand, if the questions are moving by too quickly, the group is probably not discussing each one thoroughly enough. Slow down. Encourage people to interact with each other's ideas. Be sure they are working through all aspects of the question.

Then end—on time. Many people have other obligations immediately after the study and will appreciate a predictable closing time.

3. Read the passage aloud by paragraphs—not verses. Verse-by-verse reading causes a brief pause after each verse and breaks the flow of narrative, thereby making it harder to understand the total picture. So read by paragraphs.

4. Ask, don't tell. This study guide is designed for a discussion moderated by a leader. It is *not* a teacher's guide. When you lead the group, your job is like that of a traffic director. You gauge the flow of discussion, being careful that everyone gets a turn. You decide which topics will be treated, in what order. You call a halt now and then to send traffic in a new direction. But you do not mount a soapbox and lecture.

Your job is to help each person in the group personally discover the meaning of the passage and share that discovery with the others. Naturally, since you have prepared the lesson in advance, you will be tempted to tell them all you've learned. Resist this temptation until others have had a chance to discover the same thing. Then, if something is still missing, you may add your insight to the collection.

5. Avoid tangents. The bane of any discussion group is the oh-so-interesting lure of a tangent. These are always time consuming and rarely as profitable as the planned study. A few red flags will warn you that a tangent is about to arise. They are: "My pastor says . . ."; "I read that . . ."; "The other day Suzie . . ."; "If we look at Ezekiel (or John, or Revelation) . . ."

If this occurs, politely listen to the first few sentences. If these confirm your suspicion that a tangent is indeed brewing, thank the person, then firmly but kindly direct attention back to the passage.

A leader does, however, need to be sensitive to pressing needs within a group. On rare occasions the tangent grows out of a need much more important than any preplanned study can meet. In these cases, whisper a quick prayer for guidance, and follow the tangent.

6. Talk about application. Each study in this guide leads to a discussion that applies the passage to real life. If you are short of time or if your group feels hesitant to talk about personal things, you'll entertain the thought of omitting these questions. But if you do, your group will lose the main purpose of the study. If God's Word is a book to live by, a few people in your group ought to be willing to talk about how they are going to live in response to it. Putting those intentions into words will strengthen their ability to live out the teachings. The listeners will be challenged to do the same.

So always allow adequate time to talk over the application questions. Be prepared also to share your own experiences as you have tried to live out the passage.

7. Try a prayer and share time. Many groups start their session with fifteen minutes of coffee, then allow a short time of sharing personal concerns, needs, and answers to prayer. Afterward, the group members pray briefly for each other, giving thanks and praise, asking together that God will meet the needs expressed. These short, informal sentence prayers are much like casual conversation. The group members simply turn their conversation away from each other and toward God. For many, this brief time of prayer becomes a weekly life line.

8. Enjoy leading. It's a big responsibility, but a rewarding one.

BIBLE STUDY SCHEDULE

Date	Passage	Leader	Hostess
	Genesis 2:15−3:24		
	Romans 3:9−26		
	Luke 15		
	Acts 3; Isaiah 53		
	Ephesians 2:1−10		
	John 3:1-21		
	Luke 14:25−33; Romans 10:9−12		
	1 Corinthians 15		
	Luke 11:1−13		
	Psalm 19		
	1 Corinthians 12		
	Galatians 5:13−26		

Names and phone numbers:

PLEASE CALL HOSTESS IF YOU CANNOT ATTEND

1

WHY DO I FEEL THAT GOD IS FAR AWAY?

Genesis 2:15–3:24

Why is it that though the preachers tell us that God is present everywhere, we hardly see Him anywhere? Wars go on unhindered. Crime statistics mount. Children die of leukemia. Even our own prayers seem to rebound from off our bedroom walls.

Is there really a great gulf between God and humanity? Or is this feeling of distance only in our heads? Was it always that way? And will it always be? Can anything be done about it? Who can bridge the gap? And how?

To find out how that uneasy feeling began, we begin at the beginning: in Genesis, with one man and one woman—and God.

Read aloud Genesis 2:7 and 15–25.

1. What seems inviting about this picture of the Garden of Eden? (Would you like to live there? Why?) _____

---

2. Look carefully at verses 16 and 17. To whom was God speaking? _____

   What did He permit? _____

   What did He prohibit? _____

   Why? _____

3. What value was it to Adam to view the animals in the way that he did? _____

   _____

   What value was it to the animals? _____

   _____

   What value would it be to Adam's future wife? _____

   _____

   _____

4. Look again at verses 21–24. What benefits might the woman reap from this particular method of creation?

   _____

   _____

   _____

5. Why do you think words from this passage are so frequently quoted in today's wedding ceremonies? ____

   _____

   _____

6. Review your study so far. In what ways did God show His personal concern for the man and the woman He had made? _____

   _____

_____

_____

_____

_____

_____

Read aloud Genesis 3:1–13.

7. What mixture of truth and lie did the serpent combine in his temptation? _____

_____

_____

8. What ingredients led to the woman's yielding to the serpent's trickery? _____

_____

_____

_____

9. What exactly did she do wrong? _____

What inner attitudes did this reflect? _____

_____

_____

_____

10. Because of this action, what changes occurred in the sensitively balanced relationships between the major characters in this account?

Adam and Eve? _____

_____

People and God? _____

_____

People and animals? _____

_____

Read aloud Genesis 3:14–24.

11. What drastic changes occurred in God's creation because of this first sin? _____

_____

_____

12. Look more carefully at each of the three curses. What
notes of mercy do you find in each? _____

_____

_____

_____

13. How might God's driving Adam and Eve out of the Garden of Eden be viewed as a mercy as well as a punish-
ment? _____

_____

_____

14. Think back over the entire section of Scripture you
studied today. Why do you think God values obedience
to His commands so highly? _____

_____

_____

_____

_____

15. What explanations does this account suggest for the uneasy feeling so many of us have that a great gulf separates humankind from God? _____

_____

_____

_____

16. What hope can you offer for bridging that gulf? _____

_____

_____

_____

2

BUT I TRY TO BE GOOD
(MOST OF THE TIME)

Romans 3:9–26

I'm a pretty good person. I don't lie. I don't cheat. I see that my children are well fed, well clothed, and well disciplined. I babysit for my neighbor's kids. I help out at school and work to solve community problems. I make an honest effort to understand the people around me and treat them as I would want to be treated. I'm a good citizen, a good parent, and a good friend. Isn't that good enough for God?

Read aloud Romans 3:9–20.

1. Compare the mood you feel in this passage with the mood you sensed in Genesis 2:15–25. _____

   _____

   _____

   Why do you think the tone is so different? _____

   _____

   _____

2. Find words and phrases in this selection from Romans that describe all people. _____

_____

_____

_____

3. Look again at verses 13–18. Why would Paul describe in this way human bodies created by God? _____

_____

_____

4. What specific wrong uses of the body do you think he had in mind? _____

_____

_____

5. According to these verses, what are some of the major purposes of God's law? _____

_____

_____

What can the law not do? _____

_____

6. If you were to end your study of *New Life* at this point, what would you conclude? _____

_____

_____

What would you hope for? _____

_____

_____

Read aloud Romans 3:21–26.

7. What hope does this paragraph offer in our quest for new life? _____

_____

_____

8. Look again at verse 23 and think about Genesis 2. In what ways did man and woman, as God created them, reflect the "glory of God"? _____

_____

What does verse 23 add to the view of the current state of humankind that Paul had already expressed in verses 11–18? _____

9. Pause for a moment of silent meditation. Ask God to show you specific ways in which your thoughts and actions "fall short of the glory of God."

10. What information does this paragraph (verses 21–26) provide about God's righteousness? Find all that you can. _____

_____

_____

_____

_____

11. In what sense does Christ's "sacrifice of atonement" (verse 25) demonstrate God's justice? _____

_____

_____

12. In view of these verses, how do you think Paul would respond to the person who says, "I'm a pretty good person. Surely God would not turn me away"? _____

    _____

    _____

    _____

13. According to this passage, why does a person need atonement? _____

    _____

    How does he or she receive it? (Notice the words and phrases that tell how.) _____

    _____

    _____

14. If you were to admit, based on these first two studies, that you are in fact sinful and need to be made right with God, what avenues would you want to explore next?

    _____

    _____

    _____

3

JESUS LOVES ME?

Luke 15

Sometimes the best way to teach a truth is to tell a story. Wherever Jesus went, a certain group of detractors followed. They were the Jewish religious leaders, the Pharisees. They were troubled by this upstart teacher who refused to stay within the tightly protected circle of Jewish legalism. Instead, He openly "welcomed sinners."

So Jesus told the Pharisees three little stories: parables about a shepherd and a homemaker and a father. And in so doing, Jesus talked about Himself.

Read aloud Luke 15.

1. What does the Pharisees' complaint reveal about their own attitudes? _____

   _____

2. Look again at verses 3–7. What do you learn about the shepherd in this parable? _____

_____

_____

_____

3. Put yourself for a moment in the mind of the one sheep. What was it thinking and feeling at various points in the story? _____

_____

_____

_____

What larger events could the sheep not see? _____

_____

_____

4. Look again at verses 8–10. What ingredients does this parable of the coin have in common with the parable of the sheep? (Find all that you can.) _____

_____

_____

_____

5. Note particularly the explanation of the parables in verses 7 and 10. What brings about the rejoicing? ____

_____

Where does it occur? _____

Who rejoices? _____

What does it tell you about the way God views repentance? _____

_____

What does this picture of heaven, unknown to a sheep and a coin, hint about your own value before God?

_____

_____

6. Focus on verses 11–32. What steps led the younger son to "come to his senses"? (Begin at the beginning.) _____

_____

_____

_____

7. When he arrived at this point, what did he realize about himself? _____

_____

_____

8. If you had been the father, what would you have said and done when you saw your destitute son headed toward home? _____

_____

_____

9. Find as many ways as you can in which the father demonstrated his love to this son. _____

_____

_____

_____

_____

10. Now look at the older brother. In what ways did he display his anger? _____

_____

_____

_____

11. What clues can you find that the father loved this son also? _____

_____

_____

12. What attitudes prevented the older brother from experiencing the same kind of relationship with his father that the younger son now enjoyed? _____

_____

_____

13. What do you think the father meant when he said, "This son of mine was dead and is alive again"? _____

_____

_____

14. Think about the actions of the sheep, the coin, and the younger son. In what ways were they similar? _____

_____

How were they different? _____

_____

What does this lead you to believe about the condition of those who are "found" by Jesus? _____

_____

_____

15. How might these three parables help you believe that Jesus loves you? _____

_____

_____

_____

_____

4

REPENT? YOU'VE GOT TO BE KIDDING!

Acts 3
Isaiah 53

Dust, ashes, and hair shirts. Ancient symbols of repentance aren't likely to attract many followers today. We're more into building a positive self-image and "affirming" each other with "warm fuzzies" or a hearty pat on the back. Saying "I was wrong. I have sinned," even to God, sticks in twentieth-century throats.

But all is not well in this twentieth-century Eden of mental health. We can so industriously cover a nagging guilt with Positive Mental Attitude that we never experience the relief of God's genuine forgiveness. Dust, ashes, and hair shirts we can do without. But to receive forgiveness, repentance is a must ingredient.

Read aloud Acts 3:1–10.

1. What does this account let you know about each of the major characters:

Peter? _____

_____

_____

John? _____

_____

_____

The lame man? _____

_____

_____

2. How did each of these people direct attention away from himself? _____

_____

_____

_____

Read aloud Acts 3:11–16.

3. What use did Peter seem to want to make of the crowd's excitement over this miracle? _____

_____

_____

4. Notice Peter's use of the word "you." Why were these statements unlikely to have made Peter a popular person with this audience? _____

_____

_____

_____

5. In what different ways might Peter's hearers have responded to these accusations? _____

_____

_____

_____

_____

6. Notice the titles Peter used for Jesus in verses 14–15. What do these titles imply that Peter believed about Jesus? _____

_____

_____

_____

What evidence did Peter offer that the "author of life" was no longer dead? _____

_____

_____

_____

Read aloud Acts 3:17–26.

7. Peter conceded that, in killing Jesus, the people acted out of ignorance. According to Peter, what should they have known about their promised Christ? _____

_____

_____

_____

_____

_____

8. Isaiah 53 is an example of prophetic writings about Christ. Read this chapter aloud. How could this chapter have helped Jewish people correctly identify Christ?

_____

_____

_____

_____

9. What does this chapter contribute to your own understanding of Christ and His purposes? _____

_____

_____

_____

_____

10. Look again at Acts 3:17–26. According to these verses, what future events surrounding Christ can we still anticipate? _____

_____

_____

_____

11. What does this chapter suggest as the appropriate response of a person who encounters Jesus Christ? _____

_____

_____

12. Look carefully at verses 19 and 26. What does Peter say is involved in true repentance? _____

_____

_____

What can a person who repents expect to happen as a result? _____

_____

13. What is hard about repentance? _____

_____

_____

_____

14. Look again at all of the references to God and to Jesus Christ in this chapter. Notice also the characteristics of those whose lives He touched. What information here might influence you to do as verse 19 says: "Repent and turn to God"? _____

_____

_____

_____

_____

_____

_____

5

CAN I WORK MY WAY TO HEAVEN?

Ephesians 2:1–10

Picture the scene in heaven: God, looking like an old man with a beard, holds a balance scale in His hands. One side is labeled good. The other, bad. You stand before Him. Bit by bit you deposit your small offerings. Babysitting for a sick neighbor: good. A white lie to your mother-in-law: bad. And so it goes. In the end, if the good outweighs the bad, you've earned your way to heaven. If not—good-by.

It's a commonly held myth. But not a shred of Scripture supports it. Look instead at what the apostle Paul says about the place of good works.

Read aloud Ephesians 2:1–3.

1. Describe the problem Paul presents here. _____

_____

_____

_____

2. In describing anyone so obviously lively, why would Paul begin by saying, "You were dead"? _____

_____

_____

_____

3. What do you know from your studies thus far of new life that would help you understand what Paul means when he says in verse 3, "Like the rest, we were by nature objects of wrath"? _____

_____

_____

_____

4. Notice the phrase, "All of us" (verse 3). Survey again the kind of people described in these three verses. What problems can you foresee if a person of this description tried to work his or her way to heaven? _____

_____

_____

_____

_____

Read aloud Ephesians 2:4–10.

5. Who is the active person in this section in contrast to the active person in the first section? _____

_____

_____

_____

What reasons can you see for this change in who is active? _____

_____

_____

6. What characteristics of God are evident in verses 4–10?

_____

_____

_____

_____

Why is each of these characteristics important in view of the situation described in verses 1–3? _____

_____

_____

_____

_____

7. According to these verses, what actions does God take to solve the problem described in verses 1–3? _____

_____

_____

_____

8. Notice the mixture of present, past, and future in verses 4–10. What events in the future of a Christian are so certain that Paul speaks as if they had already happened?

_____

_____

What does this hint about the nature of this gift Christ offers? _____

_____

_____

9. In view of the first three verses, what does Paul mean when he says in verse 5, "You have been saved"?

_____

_____

_____

_____

_____

10. Look more carefully at verses 8–10. What is the difference between the "works" of verse 9 and the "works" of verse 10? _____

_____

_____

_____

_____

11. Why might a confidence in your own good works keep you from being saved? _____

_____

_____

_____

_____

_____

12. Why might some people feel a reluctance to receive this kind of gift from God? _____

_____

_____

_____

What do you find appealing in the way God offers this gift? _____

_____

_____

6

WHAT'S ALL THIS "BORN AGAIN" STUFF?

John 3:1–21

When reporters questioned presidential candidate Jimmy Carter about his religious orientation, he answered, "I have been born again." And suddenly this rather paradoxical term made headlines everywhere. Some politicians claimed it, others ranted against it, comedians made fun of it. In no time, the public, even those who never attended church and didn't possess a Bible, knew personally someone who also claimed to have been born again. Often the response to new birth was more a reaction to the person who claimed it than to any precise understanding of what the whole idea meant.

Though *born again* is new to the headlines, it is an ancient term. Jesus used it in a private conversation with a Jewish religious leader named Nicodemus.

Read aloud John 3:1–3.

1. What preliminary steps had Nicodemus taken that might have helped him be receptive to Jesus? _____

43

_____

_____

_____

_____

_____

2. What reasons did Nicodemus have to be surprised at Jesus' response to his visit? _____

_____

_____

_____

3. What ideas does the term "born again" bring to your mind? _____

_____

_____

Read aloud John 3:3–15.

4. What words and phrases indicate that being born again is important? _____

_____

_____

5. What patterns from nature did Jesus use to help Nicodemus understand? _____

_____

_____

What spiritual truths do these natural happenings illustrate? _____

_____

_____

6. What comparisons did Jesus draw between Israel's teachers and His own authority? _____

_____

_____

_____

7. Look up Numbers 21:6–9. How might this incident in Jewish history help Nicodemus understand Christ and His message? _____

_____

_____

_____

Read aloud John 3:16–21.

8. Look more carefully at John 3:16. Many theologians call this verse "the Christian message in a nutshell." What can you know of Christianity from this verse? Find all that you can. _____

_____

_____

_____

_____

_____

_____

9. According to this paragraph (verses 16–21), does a person start out right or wrong with God? _____

   Why? _____

   _____

   In what two ways can a person respond to Jesus? _____

   _____

   _____

   What is the result of each of these two responses? _____

   _____

   _____

10. What reasons did Jesus give for why a person might choose not to believe in Him? _____

    _____

    _____

11. What is comfortable about darkness in a physical sense?

    _____

    _____

    In a spiritual sense? _____

    _____

    _____

12. Christianity has sometimes been criticized as a "one way gospel." What evidence can you find in this chapter to support that claim? _____

    _____

    _____

    _____

_____

_____

_____

13. Why might this claim to "the truth" (verses 3 and 21) be offensive to some but a joy to others? _____

_____

_____

_____

14. If what Jesus says in John 3 is "the truth," how must a person come into right relationship with God? _____

_____

15. Why might this change seem like new birth to someone who has lived in spiritual darkness? _____

_____

_____

_____

7

DECISION TIME:
WHAT'S IT GOING TO COST ME?

Luke 14:25–33
Romans 10:9–12

You've spent weeks in a realtor's car combing the country-side for the perfect house. Finally you've found it: nestled among tall trees and with a view of the sunset. The room arrangement is practical. The basement is just right for your husband's hobbies. The kitchen even has a dishwasher. You can already picture your family snug and happy in this setting. It's time to sit down at the realtor's desk and sign the papers.

But wait. You must make one final consideration: What will it cost? Taxes, principle, interest, utilities, decorating, moving expenses. To fail here might lead to financial ruin.

So it is with new life. Christ's gift of salvation is free. But it is not without cost. Because this free gift will result in some important changes in life's pattern, a wise person will first study the cost before making any decision.

Read aloud Luke 14:25–27.

1. According to these verses, what is the cost of becoming a disciple to Jesus Christ? _____

48

_____

_____

_____

_____

Note: The word "hate" (verse 26) means "love less" (New Bible Commentary, p. 911). See Matthew 10:37–38 for its use in a similar context.

2. Since the cross was a symbol of execution in this era of Roman rule, how did Jesus mean that His disciples must view themselves? _____

_____

_____

_____

3. What would be hardest for you about making this kind of commitment? _____

_____

_____

Read aloud Luke 14:28–33.

4. Why are a builder and a king good examples of people who must estimate cost before they take action? _____

_____

_____

_____

5. What spiritual harm do you think might occur if a person wanted to believe on Jesus, but did not first weigh the cost of belonging to Him? _____

_____

_____

_____

Read aloud Romans 10:9–12.

6. What part does the heart and the mouth play in salvation? (What must you believe? What must you confess?)

_____

_____

7. Why do you think that the Scripture says a belief in Christ's resurrection is necessary to salvation? _____

_____

_____

_____

8. If you were to say, "Jesus is my Lord," and mean it, what effect would it have on your day-to-day actions? _____

_____

Thinking? _____

_____

Feelings? _____

_____

9. These verses say that our confession of faith must be verbal. Why is it important to talk about what we believe? _____

_____

_____

_____

10. What assurance does this passage offer that God will accept a person who takes these steps? _____

    _____

    _____

11. Read aloud the "ABC Path to New Life" (p. 48). This forms a summary of the Scriptures we have studied together. As you read, put a check mark next to each step you have taken at some time in the past.

12. Now take a few moments privately to check the appropriate box below.

    ☐ 1. I have taken all of these five steps in the past. Therefore I can know that God has placed me in His family and given me life forever with Him.

    ☐ 2. I have not taken all of these steps in the past. The following steps are missing: A B C D E (circle those appropriate). With God's help, I am now taking those missing steps.
    Write the name of one person you will tell of this decision. _____

    ☐ 3. I have not taken all of these steps in the past, but I want to study this further before making a decision. Write the name of one person you will ask to assist you in that study. _____

    ☐ 4. I have decided not to receive new life at this time.

    When you have finished writing, spend a few moments in silent prayer about the spiritual position you have marked.

13. Now pray aloud one sentence telling God some of your thoughts about the spiritual position that you marked.

14. Take some time to share the results of this study with others in your group. Look back at what you checked on question 12.

    If you checked number 3, what factors would you like to study further? _____

    _____

    _____

    _____

    If you checked number 2, what changes do you anticipate as a result of your decision today? _____

    _____

    _____

    _____

    If you checked number 1, what are you especially thankful for about your new life in Christ? _____

    _____

    _____

    _____

8

HOW WILL IT ALL END?

1 Corinthians 15

But what difference will it make if I am a Christian, or if I am not a Christian? Even if I live until I'm ninety, so what? A hundred years later no one will ever know I existed, let alone whether I belonged to Jesus Christ. Or will they?

The Bible says that God has a special future for His people. It has something to do with Jesus Christ, raised from the dead, the "firstfruits." In God's Book, the end is merely the beginning.

Read aloud 1 Corinthians 15:1–11.

1. When Paul reminded the Corinthians of the gospel on which they had taken a stand, what words stand out as basic beliefs? (See especially verses 3–5.) _____

_____

_____

_____

Why are each of these words important to the Christian creep? _____

_____

_____

_____

_____

_____

2. What evidence did Paul offer first-century Christians who might have begun to doubt Christ's resurrection? _____

_____

_____

Read aloud 1 Corinthians 15:12–19. Circle the word "if" each time Paul uses it to question whether the dead are raised.

3. If people who are dead do not live again, what would be the results? Find all that you can from these verses.

_____

_____

_____

_____

4. If it were true that there is no life after death, why would a Christian deserve pity? _____

_____

_____

_____

_____

Read aloud 1 Corinthians 15:20-34.

5. In what sense is Christ "the firstfruits"? _____

_____

_____

_____

6. What future events does this passage detail? _____

_____

_____

_____

_____

_____

_____

7. How might this revelation of the future help you to worship God? _____

_____

_____

_____

8. Paul says in verse 33, "Do not be misled. . . . Come back
   to your senses," a plea to return to their former faith in
   the resurrection. (See verses 11–12.) What effect would a
   belief, or lack of belief, in the resurrection have on behavior? _____

_____

_____

_____

_____

Note: "Baptized for the dead" (verse 29). The Greek text may also be translated "baptized because of the dead." *The dead* may refer to Jesus Christ, or it might refer to Christian friends who had died but before their deaths had influenced others to follow them in faith and baptism. Therefore, these new converts were baptized because of their dead friends. And they hoped that they would someday be resurrected together.

9. When you visualize a resurrection from the dead, what problems come to your mind? _____

_____

_____

_____

Read aloud 1 Corinthians 15:35–58.

10. What does the example of a seed contribute to your understanding of life after death? _____

_____

_____

_____

_____

11. What two sources of life does Paul point out? (See verses 44–49.) _____

_____

What do we inherit from each? _____

_____

_____

_____

_____

Note: "Last Adam" (verse 45) is Jesus Christ.

12. According to Paul, how will life, as we know it, end?

_____

_____

_____

_____

13. Look again at verses 55–58. What does Paul suggest are natural outgrowths of the Christian view of resurrection?

_____

_____

14. If you were to encounter a period of wavering faith, how might this chapter help you stand firm? _____

_____

_____

_____

_____

15. If this belief in the resurrection motivated you to give yourself "fully to the work of the Lord," (verse 58) what specific influences would you see on your own work and service? _____

_____

_____

_____

_____

9

WHY PRAY?

Luke 11:1–13

You sit in your favorite chair, Bible open on your lap, and wait to feel like praying. Nothing. You try a few words to God, but they stumble past your lips and fall limply onto your lap. And already your mind wanders to your next job for the day.

If this situation sounds familiar, then you can understand why I've asked myself these questions: What should I do when God seems far away and when prayer seems like an empty exercise of talking to myself? Is prayer a command or an invitation? Or both? And why does God tell me to pray? Is it for His benefit or mine? Or does God choose, for reasons known only to Him, to work through the avenue of my prayers?

Whatever the answers to these questions, Scripture speaks of prayer as part of a normal Christian life. It is a route to personal growth. Even Christ's first followers, the twelve disciples, asked Jesus to teach them to pray. And He did. We might well do the same.

1. What is hard for you about praying? _____

_____

_____

_____

Read aloud Luke 11:1–4.

2. What prompted the disciples' request in verse 1? _____

_____

_____

_____

3. Examine each phrase of the model prayer in verses 2–4. What does each phrase illustrate about good praying?

_____

_____

_____

_____

_____

_____

Which of these areas in Christ's prayer are you most likely to omit from your praying? _____

_____

_____

Note: Luke gives here an abbreviated version of The Lord's Prayer. The complete prayer appears in Matthew 6:9–13.

4. Look at the story in verses 5–8. What elements of the story would make it familiar to Christ's listeners? _____

_____

_____

_____

In what ways can you relate to the story? _____

_____

_____

_____

5. How is God like the sleeping friend? How is He different? _____

_____

_____

6. Study verses 9–10. What do these verses contribute to our understanding of God? _____

_____

_____

What do they suggest that God wants from His people?

_____

_____

7. Look again at verses 11–13. What does our own experience with parent-child love teach us about God?

_____

_____

_____

8. Assume that each paragraph in today's text is part of Christ's answer to the request of verse 1, "Lord, teach us to pray." What did the disciples learn that helped them to pray? _____

_____

_____

_____

9. Let each person in your group read one of these texts aloud, then answer the following question about it: If you were to put the principle taught here into practice, how would it affect your praying this week?

2 Chronicles 7:14   Philippians 4:6
Psalm 34:15   1 Thessalonians 5:17–18
Isaiah 65:24   1 Timothy 2:8
Jeremiah 33:3   Hebrews 4:16
Acts 27:35   James 1:5
Romans 8:26   James 5:16

_____

_____

_____

_____

_____

_____

_____

10. If you don't feel like praying, should you pray anyway? Why or why not? (Draw on the Scriptural teachings of today's study for your answer.) _____

_____

_____

11. Share with your group one practice that has enriched your praying. _____

_____

12. What attitude or practice from today's study would you like to incorporate into your praying? _____

_____

_____

_____

10

SCRIPTURE: IT'S ALIVE!

Psalm 19

The Bible: a document composed of many documents—all of them ancient. Some are two thousand years old, others three thousand years old, and still others were recorded from oral tradition told from father to son before time had accurate measure. What can intelligent, well-educated, twentieth-century people have to do with a book that hasn't been updated for two thousand years?

Yet perfectly ordinary people today govern their lives by Scripture. Perfectly intelligent scholars spend fifty years studying it. Even those who are "imperfect"—the sick, the poor, the troubled—also hold to Scripture and confess that the Bible makes their day brighter.

What makes the Bible so enduring? Today's study examines how Scripture itself would answer that question. Once we've encountered that, we must also look at our response to a Book that claims it's alive.

1. What do you find difficult about studying Scripture? ____

_____

_____

Read aloud Psalm 19:1−6.

2. What different forms of communication do you see in verses 1−6? _____

_____

_____

_____

3. What links do you see here between God and these works of nature? _____

_____

_____

4. What visual pictures does David, the psalmist, paint of the sun? _____

_____

_____

   In what ways is God like the sun He created? _____

_____

_____

_____

Read aloud Psalm 19:7−11.

5. What words does David use to describe God's words?

_____

_____

_____

_____

_____

_____

6. What reasons for becoming familiar with God's Word does David give? _____

_____

_____

_____

_____

7. According to these verses, what does Scripture reveal about God that creation alone cannot reveal? _____

_____

_____

_____

8. Compare your feelings about Scripture with the psalmist's. In what ways are your feelings similar? How are they different? _____

_____

_____

_____

9. What is the difference between errors, hidden faults, and willful sins? _____

_____

_____

_____

How can a knowledge of Scripture help you resist each
of these? _____

_____

_____

_____

Read aloud Psalm 19:14.

10. In his last stanza, David turns his writing from reflection
on God's words to his own words. Meditate for a
moment on verse 14. In what ways does this stanza
express your own worship? _____

_____

_____

_____

11. Assign one of the Scripture passages below to each
group member. Have that person read it aloud and
answer the following question: If you were going
through a time of lagging interest in Scripture, how
would this passage influence you?

Numbers 23:19	Isaiah 40:8
James 1:22–25	1 Peter 1:24–25
Psalm 1:1–2	Psalm 119:105
Hebrews 4:12	Proverbs 13:13
2 Timothy 3:14–16	1 Thessalonians 2:13
Colossians 3:16	Revelation 22:18–19

_____

_____

_____

_____

_____

_____

12. If you were to give Scripture a higher priority in your life, what one specific change would you make? _____

_____

_____

_____

11

THE CHURCH: REFUGEE CAMP FOR THE IMPERFECT

1 Corinthians 12

Why go to church? It fills my Sunday morning—the only day my whole family is at home. My kids think it's boring. My husband won't go. The sermon says nothing about where I live. The music is straight out of the forties. The people all wear their Sunday-morning faces, as if they'd never tell a lie or yell at their kids. Besides, I hate getting dressed up, especially on my day off. Everybody says the church is full of hypocrites. Maybe I'd be just as well off without it. Sure, I need Jesus, but I can get along without the church just fine.

Heard objections like these or said them yourself? It's tempting—those feelings that we can live the Christian life on our own without the obligation of church ties. When the apostle Paul wrote to the Greek church at Corinth, he addressed the question of whether we need a church. And if we do need one, how we can get along within one? It seems he gave the church a high priority. In fact, he called it "the body of Christ."

We might get off on the same foot with Paul if we begin by asking ourselves the question, "What's the difference between 'going to church' and being 'in a church'?"

1. Tell briefly about one negative or one positive experience you have had with a church. _____

_____

_____

_____

_____

Read aloud 1 Corinthians 12:1–11.

2. What differences does Paul point out between Christians and pagans? _____

_____

_____

_____

3. Notice the similarities and the differences described here between believers. How could both the similarities and the differences work for the "common good" within a church? _____

_____

_____

_____

_____

_____

Read aloud 1 Corinthians 12:12–20.

4. Why is a human body a good picture of how people in a church ought to relate to each other? _____

_____

_____

_____

5. Think of some practical church situations that illustrate the kind of bickering Paul describes here. _____

_____

_____

6. What reasons does Paul give for overcoming these disagreements? _____

_____

_____

_____

_____

Read aloud 1 Corinthians 12:21–27.

7. What four different kinds of people does Paul assume we will find in a church? _____

_____

_____

Describe a kind of person that you think would fit each category. _____

_____

_____

How does Paul expect the church to treat each of these four kinds of people? _____

_____

_____

8. Why does Paul believe that this is the way people in a
   church ought to treat each other? _____

_____

_____

_____

_____

9. In view of what you have studied so far, why is it wrong
   for one Christian to feel about another Christian, "I don't
   need you" (the phrase used in verse 21)? _____

_____

_____

10. Why might a person want to become a part of the kind
    of church described here? _____

_____

_____

_____

Why might a person hesitate to take that step? _____

_____

_____

_____

11. In what ways could a church like this become a refuge?

_____

_____

Read aloud 1 Corinthians 12:27–31.

12. Look again at the nine spiritual gifts of verses 8–11 and the eight gifts of verses 27–28. Select one of these or some other skill you suspect is your own gift from God. How could you better use that gift in your church for the "common good"? _____

_____

_____

13. What are some reasons believers don't become part of a church? _____

_____

_____

_____

_____

_____

How does 1 Corinthians 12 reply to each of these objections? _____

_____

_____

_____

_____

14. In view of this chapter, what is the difference between going to church and becoming part of a church? _____

_____

_____

_____

15. If you are not now in a church, what information in today's study might influence you to become part of this kind of body? _____

    _____

    If you are part of a church, what can you do to better fill your position in this "body of Christ"? _____

    _____

    _____

    _____

12

WALK IN THE SPIRIT—IT'S A DIFFERENT WAY TO LIVE

Galatians 5:13–26

Does being a Christian make any real difference? Or is it merely a written contract in which God records somewhere up in heaven "sins forgiven" yet life here below continues much the same?

We see Christians who are an irritating thorn at home or at work, and we see unbelievers who are paragons of efficient peace. Does this mean that being a Christian makes no difference. Is the converted unbeliever as mean as ever? Or is the person truly different (not better, perhaps) from a more stable (though unbelieving) neighbor, but better than she would have been without Jesus Christ and the presence of His Holy Spirit?

And what does the apostle Paul mean when he says that true believers "walk by the Spirit"? Is he hinting, perhaps, that the changes in our lives are gradual but along a steady, prescribed course? What does Paul mean when he says we are free yet we are servants?

The Christian walk is a different way to live—different from our former selves and perhaps different from our neighbors. One thing for certain—it has a wonderful growing edge.

1. What differences do you expect to see between Christians and other people? _____

_____

_____

_____

Read aloud Galatians 5:13–15.

2. What connections do you see here between freedom and service? _____

_____

_____

3. What problems might you cause the people in your life if you become obsessed with your own rights to freedom? _____

_____

_____

_____

4. How does the summary command, "Love your neighbor as yourself," draw on both freedom and service? _____

_____

_____

_____

Read aloud Galatians 5:16–26.

5. Circle in your Bible each mention of the word "Spirit" in this passage. Notice the three words preceding the word Spirit in each instance. What do these various words suggest about the nature of God's Holy Spirit? _____

_____

_____

_____

6. What conflict does Paul outline? _____

_____

_____

7. Study the "acts of the sinful nature" listed in verses 19–21. What different categories of wrong-doing do you see here? _____

_____

_____

8. As you look through this list, examine what signs in your behavior could warn you that your sinful nature is attempting to regain territory that you have given to God's Spirit. _____

_____

_____

9. Study the ninefold fruit of the Spirit. Discuss a definition for each. _____

_____

_____

_____

_____

_____

_____

_____

_____

_____

10. How would the people in your home or work place benefit if even one person there fully exercised the fruit of the Spirit? _____

_____

_____

11. If you were to pick one aspect of this fruit to emphasize in your behavior this week, which would it be and why?

_____

_____

12. In view of today's Scripture, what would you say Paul means when he says, "live by the Spirit"? _____

_____

_____

13. As you think back over today's study, what do you see as your own growing edge? _____

_____

_____

_____

ABC PATH TO NEW LIFE

Admit that I am a sinner and that my sin separates me from God.

> For all have sinned and fall short of the glory of God (Rom. 3:23).

Believe that Jesus died to pay for my sins.

> For God so loved the world that he gave his one and only Son, that whoever believes in him shall not perish but have eternal life. For God did not send his Son into the world to condemn the world, but to save the world through him. Whoever believes in him is not condemned, but whoever does not believe stands condemned already because he has not believed in the name of God's one and only Son (John 3:16–18).

Count the cost of committing to Christ all areas of my life from now on.

> If anyone comes to me and does not hate his father and mother, his wife and children, his brothers and sisters—yes,

even his own life—he cannot be my disciple. And anyone who does not carry his cross and follow me cannot be my disciple. Suppose one of you wants to build a tower. Will he not first sit down and estimate the cost to see if he has enough money to complete it? (Luke 14:26–28).

D*o it. Tell God in prayer that I repent of my sin and give myself wholly to Him.*

Repent, then, and turn to God, so that your sins may be wiped out, that times of refreshing may come from the Lord (Acts 3:19).

E*xplain what I have done to at least one person, telling him or her that Jesus is now my Lord.*

That if you confess with your mouth, "Jesus is Lord," and believe in your heart that God raised him from the dead, you will be saved. For it is with your heart that you believe and are justified, and it is with your mouth that you confess and are saved (Rom. 10:9–10).

Note: Step E is a natural result of the previous steps, one evidence that you have already received the gift of new life.

How can I know if I have new life?

Have you at any time in your past taken each of these five steps? If so you may safely assume that God has placed you into His family and granted you life forever with Him. Thank Him for this rich relationship with Himself.

How great is the love the Father has lavished on us, that we should be called children of God! And that is what we are! The reason the world does not know us is that it did not know him. Dear friends, now we are children of God, and what we will be has not yet been made known. But we know that when he appears, we shall be like him, for we shall see him as he is.

Everyone who has this hope in him purifies himself, just as he is pure (1 John 3:1–3).

But if one or more of these steps are missing from your spiritual sojourn, or if you aren't sure you have taken that path, please seriously consider taking these five steps today.

Then Jesus declared, "I am the bread of life. He who comes to me will never go hungry, and he who believes in me will never be thirsty" (John 6:35).

HELPS FOR LEADERS

1 / WHY DO I FEEL THAT GOD IS FAR AWAY?
Genesis 2:15–3:24

1. Encourage everyone present to make some response to this first question. A person will feel much less hesitant to participate in the ensuing discussion if she has already heard her own voice early in the session.

Note: Somewhere during this study, one or more people are likely to express the view that the Genesis account of creation is a myth. To become embroiled in a debate about inspiration of Scripture will be counter-productive at this point. Simply admit that many people do view Genesis this way. But explain that the purpose of your study is to discover what truths this "story" illustrates and what the writer wanted his reader to learn from it.

2. An interesting additional question, if time permits, is: What do you think God meant when He began these instructions with the words, "You are free . . ."? (v. 16).

6. Group members should note each of the following:
God's personal form of creating man (v. 7)
God's giving man work to do (v. 15)
God's strong warning to obey (vv. 16–17)
God's concern about man's loneliness (v. 18)
God's way of familiarizing Adam with his job and environment (vv. 19–20)
God's provision for a man and woman to feel comfortable together (v. 25)

8. The passage points to several ingredients that led to Eve's response:
The warning was given to Adam, not Eve (v. 16).
Her version of the command differed slightly from what God had said to Adam. (Compare Genesis 3:16–17 with 3:3.) Did Adam change it in telling Eve? Did she misunderstand him? Did Eve purposely exaggerate the command while talking to the serpent?
Notice also the attractive mixture of truth and fiction in the serpent's proposal (v. 5).
And finally, see the three steps leading to Eve's decision (v. 6).

10. Your group can spot some hints of the former relationship between people and God by reviewing verses 8 and 9.

13. God drove them from the Garden in order to keep them from living forever a life that could, after the Fall, only become more and more marred by sin. Because of this, death

could be viewed as a mercy. Notice also that God Himself clothed them in preparation for the rigors of the outside world—and that to do this, animals had to die: a prefiguring of the animal sacrifices later established by God's commands to His people, the Jews. Of course, this act also looks even farther forward to God's own death in the person of Jesus Christ.

16. The bridging of this gap is only hinted in today's passage. (See Genesis 3:15 and 21.) Some group members may point these out. Others may reply from their own knowledge and experience of the new life in Christ. Try to keep responses pointed but brief. In lessons two through eight, the group will discover together God's plan for bridging this gap.

2 / BUT I TRY TO BE GOOD (MOST OF THE TIME)
Romans 3:9–26

2. Your group should point out some of the following descriptions in text: none righteous, no one understands, no one seeks God, all have turned aside, have gone wrong, throat an open grave, tongues deceive, lips like venom, mouth full of curses and bitterness, feet swift to shed blood, wreak ruin and misery in their path, don't know the way of peace, no fear of God.

3. See verses 13–18. Paul is pointing out the sinfulness of even our physical nature. He paints sin as being both personal and ugly. The imagery makes us want to turn away from ourselves. In order to comprehend a need for redemption, we must glimpse a little of a holy God's revulsion at our sin. (These verses are quoted from various psalms.)

4. Help your group think particularly of wrongful uses of the various body parts: throats, tongues, lips, mouths, feet, eyes (minds). Don't neglect "small" sins such as lying, gossiping, overeating, hurting people by what we say.

5. See verses 19–20. Notice particularly the words "silenced," "accountable," "conscious of sin."
According to verse 20, obeying the law cannot cause anyone to "be declared righteous in [God's] sight."

7. Romans 3:21–26 contains many difficult words with complex theological meanings. Try reading these verses from Today's English Version of the Bible to help your group understand the main thrust of what Paul is saying. Treat this question briefly as details will be added in succeeding questions.

9. Allow adequate time (about three minutes) for silent prayer and meditation but do not discuss the findings. Simply continue with question 10.

10. Your group should notice that:
God's righteousness is apart from the law (v. 21).
The Law and the Prophets (Old Testament) testify to His righteousness (v. 21).
God's righteousness is provided in Christ through faith (vv. 22–25).
God's righteousness is just (v. 26).
Your group may also spot other aspects here of God's righteousness.

12. By this time women in your group should be able to express some version of the following: God will not turn away

any one who sincerely seeks Him. But a seeker must come to God, not with a sense of his or her own goodness, but with a conviction of deep personal sinfulness. Then that person will know that God cannot receive him or her on the basis of merit, but only because of Jesus Christ.

13. In a crime, justice demands that someone has to pay. Christ's "sacrifice of atonement" meets that standard of justice. If this is not readily apparent, let your group probe around in the text until they discover it.

14. Hints come out of the following words: faith (vv. 22, 25, 26), freely (v. 24), by Christ Jesus (v. 24).

3 / JESUS LOVES ME?

Luke 15

Today's study is lengthy, so start promptly and keep an eye on the clock. Allow time for important questions, but be ready to summarize those of lesser value. Pace the study so that you have about twenty minutes left for questions 13 through 15.

In order to enjoy the benefit of storytelling, divide today's reading among four fluent readers using the following divisions: verses 1–2, verses 3–7, verses 8–10, verses 11–32.

1. Refer to verses 1–2.

10. See verses 25–30.

11. Many Bible commentators conclude that the older brother represented the Pharisees who questioned Jesus in

verses 1–2. Therefore the parable is purposely left unfinished. The Pharisees themselves did not know how they would respond to the father's undiscriminating love.

12. You should have twenty minutes remaining after discussing this question.

13. If your group does not automatically enlarge their answers to interpret the parable ask, "What does this same statement mean in the larger interpretation of the parable?" They should then get into the idea of what it means for a person to be spiritually dead and the joy that would come by being made alive by Jesus Christ.

14. They are all lost, but with varying degrees of consciousness of their lostness and varying responsibility for their condition. Yet Christ redeemed them all.

15. Encourage group members to verbalize their inner feelings and to review the events in the parables that will help them believe.

4 / REPENT? YOU'VE GOT TO BE KIDDING!

Acts 3
Isaiah 53

1. Search the passage carefully, finding details that help you know the make-up of each character.

If you are not pressed for time, consider asking, "What are the indications that this miracle was not a fake?"

2. Treat each character separately noticing that Peter and the lame man both directed attention to God or Jesus Christ, while John said nothing at all.

5. Help your group think of both positive and negative reactions. Sometime during the study, they ought to figure out that Peter's listeners had to recognize their own sin in order to receive God's forgiveness.

6. In answering the first question, be sure to treat both titles for Jesus. They imply that Jesus, whom the Jews had rejected, was God Himself. As you look at the second question, notice that the evidence Peter offered for Christ's resurrection includes the idea that God (the Almighty God of Abraham) raised Him, that Peter and John were themselves witnesses of this resurrection, and that evidence of that resurrection was the lame man's healing. (A dead Jesus could hardly have performed such action.)

7. See verses 22–26.

8. Ask an expressive reader to read all of Isaiah 53 before discussing questions 8 and 9. Then work briefly with the questions. Your main time and effort should center around Acts 3.

10. See especially verses 20–21.

11. See verses 19 and 26.

13–14. Reserve about fifteen minutes to discuss these two questions. Encourage people to speak honestly about the unattractiveness of repentance, but also about the drawing power of Jesus Christ.

5 / CAN I WORK MY WAY TO HEAVEN?

Ephesians 2:1–10

1. Have your group look at the origin, scope, and characteristics of the problem.

2. In these verses, "dead" seems to indicate someone whose life is governed not by love of God but by love for self and the world. Such a person has chosen to ignore God's values and has followed other loyalties. He or she is spiritually dead.

3. Your group should remember particularly their study of Genesis 3 and Romans 3.

New Bible Commentary combines the ideas from both these passages and says of verse 3, "[We are] under divine judgment by reason of moral choice which in turn is dictated by man's warped nature" (p. 1110).

6. After pointing out several characteristics of God in response to the first part of the question, your group should deal with the second question coming to conclusions similar to these:

We need a God who is merciful, because we have been disobedient and deserve His anger. God must be loving, because if the picture of the first three verses is correct, we are quite unlovely. We need His generosity and kindness, because we have nothing to bring to Him to recommend us—we are impoverished. And we need a God who is creative, since we are dead and need to be created anew.

8. See especially verse 8.

9. You might get more accurate answers by breaking this question into smaller parts. Be sure that your group discusses, from the passage, Paul's ideas on: You have been saved from what? To what? By whom? How?

10. If your group seems confused here, have them look at the reasons for the two kinds of works. The actions of the works may turn out to be the same, but the purpose is totally different.

12. Treat each part of this question separately. Linger on it long enough for most group members to respond in one way or another.

6 / WHAT'S ALL THIS "BORN AGAIN" STUFF?

John 3:1–21

1. Answers should include:

He was a Pharisee, so he was learned in the Scriptures.

He was a member of the Jewish ruling council, so he was a religious leader.

He came at night, so he could be alone with Jesus.

He recognized that Jesus was a teacher come from God, therefore Nicodemus did not see Him as a false or merely well-informed teacher.

He was knowledgeable about Jesus' actions (miraculous signs) and believed they were done through the power of God.

2. Jesus initiated a new subject into their conversation. He did not allow Nicodemus a priority position because of his

religious rank. He even hinted that Nicodemus, himself, might be kept out of God's kingdom. In addition, Christ's message of verse 3 sounds authoritative, even exclusive.

3. Encourage everyone present to respond briefly to this question.

Plan to cover the first three questions rather quickly, since later questions will require more thorough discussion.

4. Pick out these phrases from verses 3–7:
Cannot see the kingdom of God (v. 3)
The truth (v. 5)
Cannot enter the kingdom of God (v. 5)
You *must* be born again (v. 7)

5. See verses 6–8.
"Flesh gives birth to flesh" (v. 6) says that the character of those born is determined by its source.

"The wind blows wherever it pleases" (v. 8) suggests that the miracle of new birth is beyond human control.

"You cannot tell where it comes from or where it is going" (v. 8) implies that we should expect that some spiritual truths will be beyond our understanding.

6. Let your group sort out the details of verses 10–13.

7. Compare Numbers 21:6–9 with John 3:14–15.

8. It will help if your group takes the words of this compact verse in sequence. They should make some comment on each of the following words or phrases:
God
so loved
world

gave
one and only Son
whoever believes in Him
not perish
eternal life

9-10. Treat these factual questions as rapidly as you can in order to leave time for remaining questions. But be sure the answers are accurate.

If your group is confused by 9a, point them to verse 18. They should discover that people start out wrong with God. They are "condemned already" because they have not believed.

An optional question following number 10 is: What does verse 21 suggest as the driving force behind a believer's good works? The phrases *the truth* and *through God* provide textual clues.

12. Your group should survey the passage and point out each of the following:
Cannot see the kingdom of God (v. 3)
Cannot enter the kingdom of God (v. 5)
Must be born again (v. 7)
No one has ever gone into heaven except . . . (v. 13)
One and only Son (v. 16)
Whoever believes in Him is not condemned (v. 18)
Whoever does not believe stands condemned already (v. 18)
The truth (vv. 3, 21)

13. You may eliminate this question if time is short.

14. Verse 18 says that we are "condemned already." That means we don't start out with a right relationship with God.

We start out wrong. Not just because of what we have done (as we learned in Romans 3) but because of what we have not done: believed.

This whole passage speaks of there being only one way to God. Therefore we cannot trust other gods or prophets, or even ourselves. The only way to be made right with God is through Jesus Christ (v. 16).

15. Encourage several people to answer. If your group has really learned from this study, you might notice some interesting changes from the responses to question 3.

7 / DECISION TIME: WHAT'S IT GOING TO COST ME?

Luke 14:25–33
Romans 10:9–12

4. If answers are incomplete ask, "What harm would result if each of these characters failed to do that kind of planning?"

7. For further questions to spur discussion try, "What does a belief in the Resurrection suggest about the nature of Christ? About His power? About the future of His people?"

10. See verses 11–12.

11. Read these steps and the accompanying Scriptures slowly aloud to your group. Ask them to check each step that is appropriate for them while you are reading.

Then tell them to turn back to question 12 of the study.

12. Allow several minutes for each person to privately work through question 12. Suggest that they don't need to feel uncomfortable about silence. They can use the time to think and pray. Then leave plenty of time for this silent meditation and prayer.

13. Lead into praying aloud by reading the instructions for number 13. Tell them that when it seems that all who wish to have prayed, you will say, "Amen." Then begin the group prayer by praying a one sentence prayer yourself. Be patient with long pauses between prayers. Someone may be making a weighty decision. Use this time for prayerful meditation. When all or most have prayed, close with a simple, "In Jesus' name, Amen."

14. Leave enough time for this question so that everyone can respond in some way. Suggest by your manner that a contribution will be welcomed from each person present. Then treat the three questions in order so that those who checked numbers three and two will have opportunity to speak first.

8 / HOW WILL IT ALL END?

1 Corinthians 15

1. Your group should point out the following words: Christ, died, sins, Scriptures, buried, raised, third day, appeared.
A short reason for the importance of each word is sufficient here. Several will be treated later in the study. Someone

should point out that the words *buried* and *third day* speak strongly that Jesus was really dead, not just unconscious.

2. Verses 5–8 provide a selective list of six individuals or groups who saw and recognized Jesus after the Resurrection. Two of these, James and Paul, were not even believers during Christ's ministry. In addition, Paul points out in verses 9–11, that he and all the other apostles had always preached the Resurrection as part of the Christian faith—and the Corinthians had believed it.

3. Group members should point out the following:
Christ was not raised (vv. 13, 16).
Preaching is useless (v. 14).
Your faith is useless (v. 14).
We are false witnesses about God (v. 15).
God didn't raise Christ (v. 15).
Your faith is futile (v. 17).
You are still in your sins (v. 17).
Those believers who have already died are lost (v. 18).
We ought to be pitied more than all men (v. 19).

5. See verse 20.

6. See verses 20–28.

8. Note the facts of verses 29–34. Then from these details, discuss the freedom of thought and action that stems from belief in life after death. Someone should also mention the restrictions that grow out of the certainty of judgment to come.

On the side of unbelief, your group should comment on at least the transitory pleasure of "Eat and drink for tomorrow we die."

12. Verses 50–57. "Not all sleep" (v. 51). Sleep here means to die. In other words, those who are alive at the time of Christ's return will not be left out of the transformation of resurrection. For further information about that event, see 1 Thessalonians 4:13–18.

14–15. Leave adequate time for most of your group members to enter a thoughtful discussion of these application questions.

9 / WHY PRAY?

Luke 11:1–13

1. Involve each person with this question.

2. Your group should spot two or three answers in this verse.

3. Use this question to look carefully at each phrase of the prayer. Christ addresses at least seven different areas of prayer in this model. Don't let familiarity with the prayer dull its meaning in your mind.

6. As you study these verses, help your group to look at them with the dual perspective of both parts of the question. These verses show God as more generous than the reluctant householder of verses 5–8. Indeed, Jesus seems here to assure any petitioner of a plentiful response. Yet, for some reason, Jesus says we should ask, seek, knock—all acts that we initiate and continue with persistence. Your group should discuss these and other ideas as it tries to further define God's character and what He wants from us through these verses.

8. Use this as a quick summary discussion. If your group has treated earlier questions in depth, a cursory look will suffice here. If the group has settled for shallow answers early in the study, however, people will benefit from a careful examination of the passage with this question.

9. If your group is small or if time is short, assign only as many of these references as is appropriate. Save fifteen minutes for the remaining three questions.

10. Expect points of view from both sides of this question.

11. Use this question to reflect on the entire study, not just the previous question. Aim for everyone to have at least a mental response to this question. Allow time for four or five people to express verbal intentions. Human nature makes us more likely to act on something we've actually put into words than a mere mental resolution.

10 / SCRIPTURE: IT'S ALIVE!
Psalm 19

1. Encourage several people to share their own difficulties, and perhaps a few triumphs, in their study of Scripture. Don't look for final solutions here, but rather an expression of need as you set the stage for a study of what the Scripture says about itself.

2. Comb these six verses for details. They all speak of ways in which creation reveals who God is. But different aspects of creation reveal different attributes of God. Your group should discuss these specific revelations as well as general conclusions about who God is.

3. Nature helps define who God is, yet God created nature. Help your group point out phrases that describe both of these links.

4. Concentrate on verses 4–6.

5, 6. Psalm 19 is written using a typical method of Hebrew poetry. One line makes a statement; the next line amplifies the statement. The third line begins a new statement, and so forth. Verses 7–11 are a series of these couplets. Use the first line of each couplet to discuss question 5 and the second line of the couplet to discuss question 6.

7. Use this question to compare verses 1–6 with verses 7–11. This should not be a phrase-by-phrase comparison. (You've already studied phrases in previous questions.) Instead, talk together about the concepts each of these two forms of revelation take on.

9. See verses 12–13.

10. Group members may point out several phrases from this verse that express their own worship. Among them might be: "words of my mouth," "meditation of my heart," "pleasing in your sight," "O LORD," "my Rock," "my Redeemer."

Don't settle for a mere recitation of phrases. Encourage each person to elaborate on how these phrases and the concepts behind them influence her worship.

11. Watch the clock here. You'll need a few minutes for the final questions. Encourage short explanations (and honest ones) rather than long sermons.

12. Not everyone will answer this question, but if two or three share specific plans with the group, others will benefit. What change might you make in your own use of Scripture?

11 / THE CHURCH: REFUGEE CAMP FOR THE IMPERFECT

1 Corinthians 12

1. If people get excited by this question, you could easily fill your entire time with it. Don't let that happen. Its purpose is to introduce what Scripture says about the church—not substitute for that Scripture.

Encourage several people to speak *briefly*. Try to get both positive and negative accounts of church experience—perhaps even both from the same person. Most of us have had both experiences, and it would be unrealistic to assume that church is either all good or all bad.

It's likely that not everyone will have a chance to address this question. That's okay. A sampling will show group members the similarities of their experiences.

2. See verses 1–3.

If your time is limited, omit questions 2 and 3 and begin the study at verse 12.

3. The term "common good" occurs in verse 7. It is an implied framework for the rest of the chapter, so don't let your group pass by it unnoticed. The majority of the study, however, lies in verse 12 and following. So encourage a quick summary of the similarities and differences noted in verses 4–11, then a few examples of how these might operate in a healthy way in the church, then move into the next section.

Note: Are charismatic gifts like speaking in tongues, prophecy, and miraculous powers still valid in today's churches? Members of your group will likely differ in opinion about this. The text itself does not answer the question. The charismatic gifts are simply lumped here with those less startling. If you spend a lot of time debating the pros and cons of whether these gifts are still current, you'll miss the main point of the passage.

A wise course is to admit that genuine believers come down on opposite sides of this question and that since your group probably can't settle the question in one short session, it seems best for the moment to "live and let live." Then proceed with the study.

4. Answers appear throughout this chapter, but encourage your group to draw primarily from verses 12–20 where Paul introduces the metaphor.

5. Keep answers brief but representative of the range of bickering of this nature.

6. Reasons for overcoming these disagreements appear in verses 12, 13, and 14. Your group also should not overlook the phrases "would not . . . cease to be part of the body" (verse 15) and "God has arranged the parts . . . just as he wanted them" (verse 18).

7. Your group should point out the "weaker" (verse 22), the "less honorable" (verse 23), the "unpresentable" (verse 23), and the "presentable" (verse 24). Then group members should note the different instructions Paul gives for the way each kind of person should be treated.

8. See verses 24–27.

Notice particularly Paul's name for the church in verse 27. If time permits, you may ask, "What does Paul mean when he names the church 'the body of Christ'?"

10. This is an optional question. If you use it, keep an eye on the clock as you discuss. Several other questions remain.

12. Point out again verse 7 with its purpose for the different gifts.

This is a preliminary application question. Though valuable, it does not merit as much time as the two questions following it. Save about twenty minutes, if you can, for questions 13 through 15.

13. Your group should list several reasons why believers might choose not to become part of a church. Besides the excuses listed in the chapter introduction, samples of more thoughtful objections include: The church is full of insincere people. I'm not good enough. Church life is too demanding on time and energy. The people in the church are not intellectually curious—blind faith stunts their intellectual growth.

Once several of these objections are voiced, discuss how 1 Corinthians 12 addresses these objections. You'll probably need to treat one objection at a time, and you may hear some objection that the chapter does not address—though it will touch most of them. If so, just admit the space limitation of 31 verses, and go on the next objection.

12 / WALK IN THE SPIRIT—IT'S A DIFFERENT WAY TO LIVE

Galatians 5:13–26

1. Use this question as a springboard into the discussion, but don't spend more than five minutes on it. A brief observation from each person will get you off to a good start.

2. This is an interpretive question. The relationship between freedom and service is not stated straight out in the passage. But the juxtaposition in verse 13 of the two seemingly opposite words implies a connection—since Paul says we are to be both. Let your group probe his likely meaning.

4. If your group worked thoroughly with question 2, you may have already answered this question. If so, just re-state your conclusion briefly and go on. If not, dig in now.

5. See verses 16, 17, 18, 22, 25. The wording suggested by the question is based on the NIV, RSV, and KJV texts of Scripture. Users of other translations may need to look after the word Spirit instead of before it.

6. Study especially verses 16–18. Someone should point out the phrase of verse 16, "will not gratify," suggesting that the believers are not entirely cured of the sinful nature. But he or she, led by the Spirit, will put up a battle against that sinful nature. Someone will probably also notice the phrase "not under law" in verse 18, pointing back to the freedom mentioned in verse 13.

9. Much of your study time should rest on this question. Be thorough enough to arrive at adequate definitions, still leaving enough time to discuss the application questions that follow.

12. This phrase appears in verse 16. If time is short, treat this question briefly.

13. If your group members need a definition of "growing edge," you might suggest that a growing edge is an area God is working on to help you become more like what He originally designed His people to be.